T. U. L. I. P.

Doctrinal Sermons on the
Five Disputed Points of Calvinism

T. U. L. I. P.

Doctrinal Sermons
on the
Five Disputed Points of Calvinism

by
Ben Lacy Rose

Providence House Publishers
Franklin, Tennessee

Published by
Providence House Publishers
Presbyterian Custom Publishing
P.O. Box 158, Franklin, Tennessee 37065.

For additional copies call 800-321-5692.

Contents

Introduction

A doctrine that is not preachable is not worth having. If you cannot preach it, then nobody needs it. However, for years I wondered how to preach on what are sometimes called "the five disputed points of Calvinism." Many of us in seminary learned the points by an acrostic: T. U. L. I. P.—Total Depravity, Unconditional Election, Limited Atonement, Irresistible Grace, and the Perseverance of the Saints.

In fifty years of ministry I preached on some of the points and around the others, but I finally decided to preach a series of sermons in which I would address each doctrine directly. It was very enjoyable for me and, I think, for the congregation.

These sermons were preached in the small rural church which I serve, Hebron Presbyterian Church, Manakin-Sabot, Virginia. The people seemed to appreciate my efforts—those who didn't were kind enough to say nothing!

Doctrinal preaching has been lacking in the Church for some time, and, as a result, many persons have little acquaintance with the basic structure of Calvin's theology. Some people in our churches are hungry for such instruction. This book is my report that the disputed points of Calvinism are preachable.

January 1992
Ben Lacy Rose

Chapter One

Total Depravity

A few months ago the *New York Times* carried a report of an interview with novelist and short-story writer Hugh Nissenson, author of *The Elephant and My Jewish Problem*. Nissenson was born of Jewish parents and raised in New York City. At the age of twenty-eight he was sent by *Commentary* magazine to cover the trial of Adolf Eichmann in Jerusalem. At the time he was a believing Jew. But at the trial he confronted the horrible details of the Holocaust and the brutal treatment of Jews by Nazis in Germany and in occupied France. Day after day an unending succession of eye witnesses paraded before him the atrocities that were heaped on his people. Nissenson says, "My faith in a personal God was dramatically eroded and eventually collapsed. The sense of horror, of being aware of what human beings are capable of doing to one another, marked me and changed the way I look at the human condition and the human race." He concluded by saying, "One of the things I now address again and again is the idea of the immense component of evil—of radical evil—in the human mind."

There are many persons who, like Nissenson, were surprised and shocked into disbelief by the Holocaust, and more recently by the trial of Klaus Barbie, the revelation of Stalin's calculated starvation of millions of Ukrainians, the cold-blooded murder of 4500 Polish officers at Katyn and the Cambodian holocaust of Pol Pot. The news of these unbelievable cruelties, in what they thought was a civilized world, devastated many persons just as it did Nissenson. They were shocked to discover that, when you scratch the surface of civilized man, you find a barbarian.

So, the doctrine of human depravity, neglected for so long, deserves to be revived and reaffirmed. One cannot but wonder whether if Hugh Nissenson had had a firm grip on this doctrine his faith might have survived the Eichmann trial. One who holds this doctrine will always be saddened but never surprised by the evils of which human beings are capable.

We shall examine this doctrine, giving first a definition of it, then its biblical support, and finally showing some of its useful functions.

Definition

A definition of the doctrine in simplest language is: Human nature has been and is utterly corrupted by sin so that man is totally incapable of doing anything to accomplish his salvation.

The doctrine does not mean that men are totally evil. It does not declare that there is no good at all in people. There is good in everybody. Most, if not all, people are capable of doing thoughtful and helpful things. A ruined temple will usually retain some elements of its lost beauty: a fluted column or a lovely mosaic. So, in the soul of man there remains what Augustine called "vestiges of God" and what some theologians call "common grace."

Nor does the doctrine declare that people are as bad as they might be. Some persons are more degenerate than others, but no one is as evil as he could be. Even Adolf Hitler loved little children. No soul embraces every sin, if for no other reason than that some sins exclude other sins. The sin of greed precludes the sin of luxury; and the sin of pride often checks the sin of sensuality.

Again, the doctrine does not mean that men are without conscience. There are very few persons, if any, who do not experience some feelings of remorse. When Jesus said to the Pharisees who had brought to Him a woman taken in adultery, "Let him that is without sin cast the first stone at her," we read, "When they heard that, they went away one by one, beginning with the eldest." I have often wondered why the oldest left first! At any rate, callous as these Pharisees were, none of them was without a conscience. So the doctrine does not declare that men are devoid of all admirable features.

But the doctrine does declare that all human beings are "depraved," which according to the dictionary means "marked by corruption and evil." The doctrine further declares that this condition is inherited from Adam, so that it is part of our original equipment and not something that we learn after we get into the world. We are tainted by sin from birth; our souls came to us stained— infected by a deadly virus. Further the doctrine declares that this depravity is total, meaning that it affects every department of our nature: intellect, emotions, will. A deadly virus is lodged in every organ of man's soul: in his thinking, his feeling, his doing. And this malignant disease of the soul renders him totally incapable of achieving salvation or peace without God's grace.

Those who deny this doctrine hold that mankind is basically good, but misguided—that human beings by nature are quite decent, but that the environment or the culture impose circumstances on them that lead them to unfortunate responses. This position holds that, if we would only give persons a fair chance, some good examples, enough food and clothing, a little education—then the basic goodness of every human being would manifest itself and people would live in peace with one another and with God. Over against this naive view of human nature, which is held by many Christians, the Reformed faith has historically declared the doctrine of total depravity—that every element of human nature is so corrupted by sin that no man can know salvation except by the transforming grace of God.

Biblical Support

Now let us see the biblical support for this doctrine. Jeremiah said, "The heart of man is deceitful above all things and desperately wicked" (17:9). The psalmist said, "Behold I was shapen in iniquity and in sin did my mother conceive me" (51:5). The *Living Bible* gives a better translation of that verse when it makes it read, "I was a born a sinner; yes, even from the moment my mother conceived me." Jesus acknowledged that men are devoid of the love which God requires. He said to the Pharisees, "I know you; you have not the love of God in yourselves" (John 5:42), and to His disciples He said, "Apart from me you can do nothing" (John 15:5).

But the apostle Paul, perhaps because he was so conscious of his own sin, talked more about human depravity than any other biblical writer. Paul spoke of men as being "dead in trespasses and sin" (Eph. 2:1); he said that men are "lovers of self rather than lovers of God" (2 Tim. 3:4); he declared that "the mind of the flesh is enmity with God" (Rom. 8:7); and he spoke of being cleansed from "the defilement of body and spirit" (2 Cor. 7:1). But Paul's most revealing passage is in the seventh chapter of Romans where he describes so aptly his own and every man's depravity, saying:

> I know that nothing good dwells within
> me, . . . For I do not do the good I want, but

the evil that I do not want is what I do. . . . So I find that when I want to do right, evil lies close at hand. I delight in the law of God in my inmost self, but I see in my members another law at war with the law of God, and making me captive to the sin that dwells in my members. Wretched man that I am! Who will deliver me from the body of this death?

Then the apostle shouts, "Thanks be to God through Jesus Christ our Lord"—for the victory that He is giving us.

But the doctrine of total depravity does not rest on a few scattered texts. It is basic to the central theme of the Scriptures, which is the Grace of God. The Bible is the book of God's grace—in creation and redemption. The doctrine of grace is predicated on man's inability to create himself and on the sinner's inability to redeem himself. Fallen man can no more accomplish his salvation than Adam could create himself. So God out of love created man, who then rebelled against Him. But God, moved again by love, entered into a covenant of grace with Christ the second Adam. Without the grace of God the sinner can no more leave his bondage to sin than Israel could free herself from slavery in Egypt. So, without the doctrine of total depravity, the central theme of the Bible is not understandable. If men can save themselves, God's grace is unnecessary.

Functions

Having defined the doctrine and having seen its biblical support, let us observe finally some functions of the doctrine—some uses which the doctrine serves. A remembrance of the doctrine of human depravity will do a number of things.

First, it will enable the church to keep its priorities straight. It will remind believers that the root cause of the human predicament is the corruption of human nature and that the only real solution for that is the grace of God. This doctrine should enable the church to remember that its first priority is to bring people to know the grace of God in Jesus Christ. Any church or denomination that long neglects this doctrine will eventually find that her program priorities have become distorted.

Second, a proper understanding of this doctrine prepares the believer to deal with the immense component of radical evil in human beings whenever he finds it. If this had been Hugh Nissenson's doctrine of man, he should not have lost his faith at the Eichmann trial. One who knows that there is no bottom to the depth of evil of which men are capable will be saddened but never surprised at the depth of evil to which men *do* fall. Also, knowledge of this doctrine prevents one from being devastated when someone he admires is revealed to have feet of clay.

Third, this doctrine leads one to a deep distrust of all human power, because Lord Acton was right, "Power corrupts and absolute power corrupts absolutely." Trained at Princeton by a staunch Calvinist, James Madison insisted on inserting into the structures of the American government a system of checks and balances on individual and governmental power. Because of the corruption of human nature, no man is to be trusted with too much power. Because of human depravity all human power corrupts the user—political power, economic power, the power of a gun, the power of money; even ecclesiastical power corrupts the user. And no one knows this better than the holders of this doctrine. And one of the main purposes of human governments and laws is to curb human depravity.

Fourth, the doctrine leads the believer to recognize and confess that all his own actions, without exception, spring from mixed motives. Everything we think or do or say is corrupted by sin. Whatever the deed, sin is a part of it. Unfortunately, this may lead one to suspect inordinately the motives of other people, and in this area we should proceed with caution.

Finally, and perhaps most important, this doctrine leads the believer to gratitude for the grace of God to him or her. Seeing the most hardened criminal, the believer of this doctrine will say honestly, "There but for the grace of God go I!" Recognizing our own inclination to sin, this doctrine makes us more grateful for God's amazing grace to us, because we know what we would be without that grace.

Let us, therefore, acknowledge our own sinfulness— our propensity to sin; let us confess that we are absolutely incapable of saving ourselves from its grip, and so let us throw ourselves on the grace of God made known in Jesus Christ—for apart from Him we can do nothing.

And let us say every day with Paul: "Thanks be to God who is giving us the victory through our Lord Jesus Christ."

Chapter Two

Election
Unearned and Unconditional

The *doctrine of election* sounds quite academic and esoteric, but I hope that I can make the subject quite personal and practical.

To serve as the source of our thoughts I give you two texts. The first is Ephesians 1:3-6, Paul's shout of triumphant joy:

> Blessed be the God and Father of our Lord Jesus Christ, who hath blessed us with all spiritual blessings in heavenly places in Christ: According as he hath chosen us in him before the foundation of the world, that we should be holy and without blame before him in love: Having predestinated us unto the adoption of children by Jesus Christ to himself, according to the good pleasure of his will, To the praise and the glory of his grace, wherein he hath made us accepted in the beloved.

Do you wish you could honestly say that?—that God has chosen and predestined you to be His son or daughter. Change the words "we" and "us" to read "me" and "I," so that the text reads like this:

> Blessed be the God and Father of our Lord
> Jesus Christ, who has blessed *me* with every
> spiritual blessing, even as he chose *me*,
> before the foundation of the world, that *I*
> should be holy and blameless before him in
> love, having predestined *me* in love to be
> his own child.

Do you wish you could really say that?

Well, in this sermon I want to convince you that you
can! I want you to believe that God has chosen you in
Jesus Christ; I want you, as Isaiah says (Isa. 44:5), to write
on your hand, "I am the Lord's."

We begin by observing that the Bible in this text and
in numerous other places makes it perfectly clear that
God does the choosing.

God Has Done Some Choosing

Often He chose some very unlikely persons, but God
selected them from among their peers to be His own. In
the history of mankind and in the story of biblical salvation, God did some choosing.

God chose Abraham. In the year 2000 B.C. there were
many men in the land of Ur (modern Iraq), but God
selected only Abraham. And God said to Abraham, so
Genesis tells us: "I am going to bless you, and make your
name great; I will be a God unto you, and to your descen-
dants after you; and in you shall all the families of the
earth be blessed" (Gen. 12:2-3). God did some choosing.

God chose Jacob. And a more unlikely character
hardly could be found. Abraham had two sons, and God
chose Isaac over Ishmael. And Isaac had two sons: Esau
and Jacob. God did not choose Esau, although he was the
oldest; but God selected Jacob, the younger, to be progen-
itor of God's people. Henceforth, the children of Israel

17

(*Israel* was another name for Jacob) knew themselves to be God's chosen people. And that is exactly what they were.

God did not choose the Egyptians, whose culture was far more advanced than that of the Hebrews. As the poet says: "How odd / Of God / To choose / The Jews"—yet he did. To the Hebrew people God said through the prophet Amos, "Of all the peoples of the earth, I chose you only" (Amos 3:2). And the psalmist says, "The Lord has chosen Jacob for himself, and Israel for his possession" (Ps. 135:4). God did some choosing.

In the New Testament we find too that God did some choosing. There were many devout virgins in Galilee during the reign of Augustus Caesar, but God selected only Mary, that in her womb a Son would be conceived by the Holy Spirit.

God chose the apostle Paul. Saul of Tarsus (that's what Paul was called at first) was a most unlikely choice. He was a persecutor of the church. And there were surely a score of devout Jews that day on the road between Jerusalem and Damascus, but Christ appeared only to Saul of Tarsus. God did some choosing.

But, you say, those were special cases: Abraham, Jacob, Mary, Paul. God doesn't choose ordinary persons like me. Oh yes He does. All these were ordinary people before God chose them.

Look again at the text. Paul is writing to the Christians in Ephesus. They were ordinary believers like you and me—a very unlikely lot; yet the apostle says, "God chose you." The Christians in Thessalonica too were the everyday garden variety of believers, yet Paul speaks of their election by God. "God," he says, "has chosen you to salvation" (2 Thess. 2:13). All through the New Testament believers are referred to as "the elect"—those whom God has chosen as His own. In the hymn "All Hail the Power" we sing, "Ye chosen seed of Israel's race, / Ye ransomed from the fall."

So, friends, as believers in Jesus Christ *you* are God's elect people. He chose you. And by His Holy Spirit He worked faith in your hearts. You made a decision for Him only after He had chosen you.

In Your Life God Has Done Some Choosing

God decided whether you would be a boy or a girl. He decided which genes you would inherit from each of your parents and your grandparents. On the day that you were born there were approximately 100,000 babies born somewhere in the world. Who decided that you would be born in these United States and not in Outer Mongolia? Who decided that you would be born in the twentieth century and not in the fifteenth? Who chose the womb in which you would be formed? Certainly not you. Who sent all those persons into your life: siblings, aunts, cousins, neighbors, teachers who influenced your character and shaped your personality long before you ever made any conscious decision? In your life God had made some very important choices for you long before you ever came to the age of discretion.

So, it was God who began the work of faith in your heart before you had made any conscious choices. God chose you first—to work faith in your heart. As the hymn writer says:

> I sought the Lord and afterward I knew
> He moved my heart to seek Him, seeking me;
> It was not I that found, O Savior true;
> No, I was found of thee.

Thus, the New Testament speaks of faith as a gift from God. The apostle Paul says, "By grace are you saved through faith, and that not of yourselves it is the gift of God" (Eph. 2:8). If you have faith in Christ, that faith is God's gift to you. So, you see: in your life God has done some choosing. By your faith in Jesus Christ you are one of God's elect. He selected you to work faith in your heart.

Is there any way to confirm this? Is there anything that will corroborate—will authenticate—God's choice of you? Yes, there is. And that brings us to our second text, 2 Thessalonians 2:13. Paul writes to the believers in Thessalonica:

> God hath from the beginning chosen you to salvation through sanctification of the Spirit and belief in the truth.

Two Marks of Election

Sanctification and belief in the truth are the two marks of election. Read the text again: "God has chosen you to salvation through sanctification of the Spirit and belief in the truth." Where sanctification and belief are present, one can be sure that election by God has preceded them.

The first mark of election is *sanctification by the Holy Spirit.* Sanctification does not mean perfection. We are not perfect—yet. Perfection is the end, and it will not be ours until we get to heaven. Sanctification is the process through which the Holy Spirit is bringing us to perfection. Sanctification is the struggle to do right. Sanctification is the striving, yearning endeavor for moral purity. Sanctification is the struggle to grow into the likeness of Jesus Christ. And all that is the work of God's Holy Spirit in us.

When I was pastor of churches in eastern North Carolina, I contended with but greatly admired the Primitive

Baptists, and there were many of them in that section. There are not many of that denomination in this area. They claim to be the original Baptists from whom the others split-away back in the eighteenth century. Those whom I knew were almost without exception solid, honest, upright folk, and they were strong believers in the doctrine of election. There was a couple in the community; the husband was a member of my Chinquapin Presbyterian Church and the wife was a member of the Muddy Creek Primitive Baptist Church. When the wife died, the husband asked the preacher of her church to conduct the funeral, and he asked me to assist. I shall never forget what that Primitive Baptist minister said of the woman who was deceased. "In this woman," he said, "we saw the struggle for righteousness; we saw her striving, longing, praying for godliness in her life. That earnest continuing endeavor (he said) was clear testimony to the Spirit's work in her—was conclusive evidence that she was one of God's elect."

He was right! Right that she was a good and godly woman who loved the Lord; and right too that the process of sanctification is one of the sure marks of a person's election.

The second identifying mark of election which Paul gives in the Thessalonian text is *belief in the truth.* Whoever believes God's truth, whoever believes in Jesus Christ—God's Spirit is at work in him or her and *that* faith is proof-positive that God has chosen that one to salvation.

Do you believe that God's Word is true? Do you believe what the Bible says about God and about His Son, Jesus Christ? If yes, then you believe the truth. You have faith, and that faith is the title-deed of your eternal salvation, of your mansion in heaven.

The writer of the Book of Hebrews says, "Faith is the

21

substance of things hoped for, the evidence of things not seen" (Heb. 11:1). You could translate that as, "Faith is the title-deed of what you do not see."

A friend of mine bought a piece of property in Alaska. He has never been there, but he always wanted to own some land there, so he arranged with his lawyer and through a lawyer in Fairbanks, Alaska, he purchased five acres on a river in a secluded section of that state. A deed for title to the property was mailed to him—title to property he has never seen. The deed in his hand is documentation—tangible evidence—that he is the owner of property he has never seen.

Your faith—your belief in the truth—is documentation of your eternal salvation. As long as you have that deed, a mansion in heaven is yours. So, Paul says, "God chose you to salvation through sanctification of the Spirit and belief in the truth." The marks of election are sanctification and belief.

Now, friends, my time is up. The doctrine of election is too large to be covered in one sermon. The Lord willing, I shall preach on this subject next Sunday when we shall look at some of the happy benefits which flow to believers from this great truth.

But, before I end this sermon, I must sound a solemn warning. Both Peter and Paul follow every discussion of election with a strong exhortation to believers—as Peter puts it, "Be diligent to make your calling and election sure" (2 Peter 1:10). Paul, after the passage from Ephesians (our first text) says, "I, therefore, beseech you that you walk worthy of the calling to which you have been called" (Eph. 4:1).

We must never presume upon our election. The elect must give continual evidence of their election by the lives they live. Even the apostle Paul says of himself, "I keep my body in subjection, lest having preached to others, I myself should be a castaway" (1 Cor. 9:27). Let the knowledge of your election not make you complacent or lazy or self-satisfied, but let it cause you to work ten times harder.

With that warning, let me conclude by saying that in this sermon I only wanted to convince you that, through faith in Jesus Christ, you are one of God's elect. As Paul says in the Thessalonian passage (the second text), "God has chosen you to salvation through sanctification of the Spirit and belief in the truth." So, now, you can join with Paul's shout of triumphant joy in the Ephesians text:

> Blessed be the God and Father of our Lord Jesus Christ, who has blessed *me* with every spiritual blessing, even as He chose *me* before the foundation of the world, that I should be holy and blameless before Him, having predestined *me* in love to be His child through Jesus Christ to the praise of his glorious grace, which He freely bestowed on *me.*

If *that* does not thrill your heart—if being able to say that does not excite you—then, you are *dead;* and God have mercy on your soul!!

Chapter Three

Benefits of Election

What do you expect your religion to do for you? What benefits flow from the Christian faith? We expect our religion to help make us better persons, to give us a measure of peace of mind and to strengthen us to meet life's struggles. Those are some of the benefits that can come to us from the doctrine of election, which declares that God has chosen us in Christ.

Last Sunday I preached on the doctrine of election and I said then that the subject was too large to cover in one sermon, so I would preach on it again today.

The text is 2 Thessalonians 2:13, Paul's words to the Christians in Thessalonica: "God has from the beginning chosen you to salvation through sanctification of the Spirit and belief in the truth."

Last Sunday I reminded you that *God has done some choosing.* In the Bible we learn that the Hebrew people, Abraham, Jacob, Paul and others were chosen by God, and we saw that in the New Testament believers are regularly referred to as "the elect"—chosen of the Lord. We saw too that in our own lives God has made some important choices without consulting us. He chose where we would be born, who our parents would be, what influences would be brought to bear upon us before we came to any decisions. We saw that by working faith in our hearts that God had *apparently* chosen us. Then we asked:

Is there any way to confirm our election by God? Yes, Paul gives two marks of election: (1) sanctification of the Spirit, and (2) belief in the truth. The first mark of election is sanctification by the Spirit. Sanctification is not perfection. Perfection is the goal of sanctification; sanctification is the process by which the Holy Spirit is moving us to that goal. The second mark of election is belief in the truth. If you believe the truth of God's Word; if you believe in Jesus Christ you have one of the marks of election.

Today, we shall look at the *benefits of election*, and as we do hope that we shall come to understand the doctrine of election better.

The first and primary benefit is the assurance of salvation.

The Assurance of Salvation

One of the greatest joys in this world is the knowledge that your soul is safe in the hands of God. The apostle Paul had that assurance. Writing to Timothy near the end of his life, Paul said, "The time of my departure is at hand . . . I have finished my course." Then he adds, "Henceforth there is laid up for me a crown of righteousness which the Lord, the righteous judge, shall give me at that day" (2 Tim. 4:8). The apostle Peter, writing to believers scattered throughout Asia Minor whom he called the "elect," assured them that there is "an inheritance incorruptible, and undefiled, and that fadeth not away, reserved in heaven for you" (1 Peter 1:4). Jesus said to his disciples, "In my father's house are many mansions," and "I go to prepare a place for you" (John 14:2). Paul speaks of it as a crown; Peter calls it an inheritance; Jesus calls it a mansion—whichever, there is one reserved in heaven for you, and for every believer. It is a great comfort to know that your salvation is sure, that your soul is safe in God's hands.

It is the believer's privilege to sing "Blessed assurance Jesus is mine / O what a foretaste of glory divine / Heir of salvation, purchase of God."

In the *Episcopal Prayer Book* the last item is "Articles of Religion." This is a statement of faith adopted by the Episcopal Church in the United States. Article XVII is entitled "Of Predestination and Election." It reads in part as follows:

> Predestination to life is the everlasting purpose of God, whereby He has determined to deliver from damnation those whom he has chosen in Christ and to bring them to everlasting salvation . . . . The godly consideration of Predestination and our Election in Christ is full of pleasant and unspeakable comfort to all who feel in themselves the working of God's Spirit.

This is an excellent statement of the doctrine of predestination and election.

The primary benefit of this doctrine is the comforting assurance of our salvation in Christ.

We do well to observe that the assurance of salvation is a key element of *spiritual maturity*. The person who is not sure of salvation is in a constant state of uncertainty about his soul—unsure of his relationship to God.

If you applied for entrance to a graduate school and moved to the community to begin your work, you would be unable to settle down to real study until you were sure that you had been accepted and enrolled as a bona fide student. You would be in a constant state of uncertainty, running to the registrar asking if you had been accepted. Until you were sure that you had been accepted, your work would remain tentative. Likewise, until you know (as Paul says) that you have been "accepted in the Beloved" (Eph. 1:6), until you know that your name is on that "roll up yonder," you will never settle down to the strenuous work of the Kingdom of God—your walk with Christ will be hesitant and intermittent. Tentative, conditional salvation begets uncertainty and fear.

But, when you can sing "I'm a child of the King, Hallelujah, I'm a child of the King, praise his name "—then you can put your mind and heart to learning the King's ways and doing the King's business. The first and primary benefit that comes to believers through the doctrine of election is assurance of salvation in Christ.

Another benefit—another thing this doctrine does for us is make us humble.

Genuine Humility

The doctrine of election brings genuine humility. It removes pride, because we know that we do not deserve God's election. We know that there was nothing in us that caused God to choose us. We say with the old hymn, "Nothing in my hand I bring / Simply to Thy cross I cling."

Our fathers in the faith called it "unconditional election" because it was not conditioned on any merit or goodness in us. It was *only* out of God's mercy and grace that He chose to save us. "Nothing in my hand I bring / Simply to Thy cross I cling," and the Cross is the ultimate demonstration of God's unmerited favor to sinners. So, the doctrine of election destroys pride and arrogance and removes all reliance on ourselves for salvation.

But some persons accuse us. They say we are arrogant to believe that God has chosen us. They say that it is presumptuous to declare that we *know* that we are saved. Arrogance? Yes, if you believe you are going to heaven because you deserve it. Arrogance? Yes, if you believe you have done something to earn God's grace. It *is* arrogance to believe that we were smart enough to choose God *before* He chose us. It *is* arrogance to believe that we are wise and strong enough to work faith in our own hearts. But it is *not* arrogance to say, "Nothing in my hand I bring / Simply to Thy cross I cling." Or especially to sing the second verse of that hymn, "Not the labor of my hands / Can fulfill Thy Law's demands; / Could my zeal no respite know; / Could my tears forever flow; / All for sin could not atone. / Thou must save and Thou alone."

The reason we are prone to disbelieve this doctrine is that we are not humble enough. As one commentator (*The Interpreter's Bible*, vol. 10, p. 616) puts it:

> We modern Christians often find this doctrine of election, which runs through the whole Bible, hard to understand. We are not humble enough. We have not been sufficiently disciplined by the righteousness of God. We are unmindful inheritors of eighteen centuries of Christian grace. We forget that we are adopted orphans. By nature we are not sons of God at all. We are simply sinners.

We forget that we are depraved sinners who are without any hope of salvation except in God's sovereign mercy. We reject the doctrine of election because we really believe that we can ultimately save ourselves by our own doings.

Admittedly there is a false arrogance—a misunderstanding of this doctrine. False assurance begets arrogance and spiritual pride; false assurance avoids the acknowledgment of our own sinfulness. False assurance prevents true repentance. Some folks think they are going to heaven because they do not believe they are sinners. That is real arrogance.

But true assurance—a proper understanding of the doctrine of election begets unfeigned humility, leads to regular, honest self-examination and confession of sin, and fosters diligent efforts to grow in the Christian life.

One result of this doctrine is that it destroys pride and arrogance, and fosters true humility in believers.

Now, folks, that's the *good* news. There is another benefit of this doctrine that is not so easily recognized as being salutary. From one perspective the doctrine of election is not so attractive.

The play *Fiddler on the Roof* is the story of a Jewish family in Russia in the early decades of this century. There are happy and humorous times in the family, but there is always a subtle galling persecution of them because they are Jews. In spite of their difficulties, however, the family remains faithful to their religion and to their God. But, the father, who is a delightful, sensitive, devout personality, after a particularly irritating experience of discrimination by a gentile official, looks up to heaven and says, "Lord, I know we Jews are your chosen people; but next time—choose somebody else, please." For him at that moment, there was little benefit to being one of God's chosen people.

And the catch for *us* is this: we have been chosen to *service*, not to privilege; we have been chosen to *work*, not to rest. God has chosen us to be His instruments, His witnesses, His agents. God has chosen us, if need be, to suffer for Christ's sake. We are chosen to do good works. Paul says, "We are his workmanship, created in Christ Jesus unto good works, which God hath before ordained that we should walk in them" (Eph. 2:10).

Boldness and Energy

So, the knowledge of our election makes us bold and energetic in the service of God. It makes us fearless in doing the work of God. Peter and John were told by the court, the Sanhedrin, to speak no more in the name of Jesus. But Peter replied, "Whether it be right in the sight of God to harken unto you more than unto God, judge ye, But we cannot but speak the things we have seen and heard." And the record says, "When they saw the boldness of Peter and John, . . . they marveled, and they took knowledge of them that they had been with Jesus" (Acts 4:13-20). The apostle Paul was one of the most energetic and fearless witnesses for Jesus Christ. His energy and boldness were prompted by his assurance that God had chosen and called him to witness and to suffer for Christ's sake.

In his little book *The Creed of Presbyterians*, Dr. Egbert Watson Smith says:

> Let me but feel in every commanded duty, in every needed reform, that I am but working out the purposes of Jehovah; let me but hear behind me in every battle for right the tramp of infinite reserves, and I am lifted above the fear of man and the possibility of final failure. I am inspired with divine strength and confidence (pp. 164-5).

So, in the long course of human history this doctrine has begotten its heroes and martyrs innumerable—who felt themselves chosen of God to witness, to work and to suffer.

The one who knows himself to have been chosen of God will not shrink from any *task* or grovel before any *man.* I love the picture in the Book of Genesis of old Jacob before Pharaoh in Egypt. Joseph had brought his father, Jacob, to present him in the court of Pharaoh. At the time Pharaoh was probably the most powerful man in the world. But Jacob in his rough clothes and sandals was not intimidated by the power or the splendor of Pharaoh's palace. Knowing himself to be a prince with God—chosen of the Lord, Jacob (the record says) "blessed Pharaoh." Wait. You mean: Pharaoh blessed Jacob. No, that's not what the Bible says. It says, "And Jacob blessed Pharaoh" (Gen. 47:7,10). The man who knows himself to have been chosen of God will not grovel before any man or shrink from any task, but is inspired with boldness and energy.

John Knox felt himself called of God to save Scotland for the Protestant faith. When threatened by Mary, the Catholic queen of Scotland, he replied, "Madam, I have never feared the face of clay, even though that face belonged to a queen." Martin Niemoeller, German pastor in Berlin, when Adolf Hitler tried to silence his opposition, replied, "The church, Sir, has a public influence to exercise; and no one, not even you, Herr Hitler, can take that responsibility from us." When you know yourself to be one of God's chosen, there comes a boldness and an energy—to witness, to service and, if need be, to suffer for Christ's sake.

And remember this: It is *by* our witness, *by* our service to those in need; it is by being God's instruments; it is by our suffering for Christ's sake—that we *confirm* His choice of us and make our calling and election sure.

A lot of people are playing at religion, dawdling with it as a child dawdles with food it doesn't want to eat. They worship, they pray, they read their Bibles, they work in the church only when it is convenient—which is not very often. Such half-hearted activity only confirms indecision and raises grave doubts about their calling and election.

Peter says, "Be diligent (that is, be energetic and bold) to make your calling and election" (2 Peter 2:10). And Paul says, "I beseech you, therefore, by the mercies of God, that you present your bodies a living sacrifice . . . Be not conformed to this world, but be transformed . . . that you may *prove* what is the will of God" (Rom. 2:1-2) —that you may demonstrate that God is at work in you.

These, then, are some of the benefits that flow to believers from the doctrine of election: *assurance of salvation, genuine humility,* and *boldness and energy* in witness and service and Christian growth.

That is what you can expect your religion to do for you, if you really believe. God grant that it shall be so.

Chapter Four

Atonement
Specific, Limited, Effective

If you had been a Jewish pilgrim coming to Jerusalem for the Passover feast in the seventh year of Pontius Pilate's term as governor of Judea, you would have passed, just outside the city, a place called Golgotha where the Romans held public executions. On that particular Friday you would have seen three crosses against the mid-day sky and you might have remarked to those with you, "Some ordinary criminals being executed for their crimes."

But you would have been wrong, for there was nothing ordinary about what took place there that day. Indeed, that central cross was to change the whole course of human history.

It is significant that the cross is the symbol of Christianity, for the crucifixion of Jesus Christ was one of the central events in the story of the Christian religion. And the doctrine of the Atonement, which deals with what Jesus accomplished by His death, is a key element of the Christian faith.

Jesus' death was not a happenstance. It was not an accidental interruption of God's plan for the human race. The Cross had been necessary since the sin of Adam and Eve in the garden. Jesus was "the Lamb slain from the foundation of the world" (Rev. 13:8). He came to die. He said, "The Son of Man came to give his life as a ransom for many" (Matt. 20:28). On the road to Emmaus, after His resurrection, He explained to two disciples who had been devastated by His death: "It was necessary that Christ suffer that he might enter his glory" (Luke 24:26).

But, why? Why was it necessary that Jesus die? What was accomplished by it?

The doctrine of the Atonement declares that, by the Cross, God accomplished exactly what He intended, namely: the salvation of His people, the forgiveness of their sins.

It is not my purpose here to expound some abstract theological dogma. What I want to do is convince you that on the cross Jesus paid the penalty for your sins, so that there is for you no condemnation awaiting, no wondering what will happen to you at the judgment.

Divine judgment is not a popular idea with this generation. Ninety-five percent of the American people say they believe in God, but many have no concept of sin or of God's hatred of it. For them God is a nice old man in the sky who is sad when they are bad; but He is not strict about His commandments and He is too loving to punish anybody.

But a God without law fosters lawlessness in people. A God who does not judge—a God without punishment—need not be feared, and without the fear of God every person does what is right in his own eyes, and the result is chaos.

There is a parallel between divine law and civil law. The Bible teaches that God punishes all who disobey His laws. A characteristic of divine judgment is that every sin, every infraction of God's law, must be punished. The same is true of civil law. A requirement of any court of justice is that all law-breakers are punished.

During the strike of the United Mine Workers against the Pittston Coal Company in southwest Virginia recently, there were four hundred infractions of the law by mine workers—some of them quite flagrant. Judge Donald McGlothlin laid fines on all who broke the law. When the parties came to settle the dispute, the judge was asked to drop the strike-related fines and simply forgive the offenders. Judge McGlothlin refused to do that. He said, "If a legal system is to retain its integrity, it must punish law-breakers; it cannot simply forgive four hundred willful infractions of the law and act as if they never happened."

Exactly! What would you think of a judge who regularly dismissed guilty criminals without exacting any penalty from them? You would rightly call him an unjust judge.

Even God cannot dismiss sins without requiring some penalty—not and remain a just God. If God did not punish sin, if God simply dismissed sinners with a wave of His hand, as if no crime had been committed when in truth there was—then His system of laws has no integrity and He is not just. So God must punish every infraction of His laws.

But that leaves God with a dilemma. Since we are all sinners, He must punish us. He must either impose upon us the punishment due for our sins, which is death, or He must come up with some other plan. God's dilemma is heightened by the fact that He loves us, and wants to be in relationship with us. He would like to accept us into His fellowship—but we have sinned and broken His laws.

So, how can God be just and the Justifier of them that believe in Jesus? That is the question Paul wrestles within the Book of Romans.

And here is where the doctrine of the Atonement comes in. The doctrine declares that God sent His Son to take the punishment for our sins. Since death is the penalty for sin, the doctrine declares that God's Son died in our place for our sins. On the cross God-in-Christ made atonement for the transgressions of His people. So, the old hymn is right when it says that "It was for crimes that I had done he groaned upon the tree."

Jesus said, "The Son of Man came . . . to give his life a ransom for many" (Mark 10:45). Peter said, "He bore our sins in his body on the tree" (1 Peter 2:24). The writer of Hebrews said, "Christ was offered once to bear the sins of many" (9:28). And Paul in several passages said, "Christ died for our sins" (1 Cor. 15:13) and concluded saying, "Through our Lord Jesus Christ . . . we now have received the atonement" (Rom. 5:11).

In the Old Testament there were numerous sacrifices of sheep and oxen. At the Passover feast a lamb was killed and its flesh eaten. These were all foreshadowings of Christ's sacrifice on the cross. John the Baptist pointed to Jesus and said, "Behold the Lamb of God that taketh away the sin of the world" (John 1:29). The whole system of Old Testament priests who offered bloody sacrifices and intercessions for the people was designed to point to the priestly work of Christ. The Book of Hebrews was written specifically to show that Christ, by His sacrificial death, is "our high priest forever" (6:20). Isaiah, the prophet, foresaw the atoning work of Christ and wrote, "He was wounded for our transgressions; He was bruised for our iniquities; the chastisement of our peace was upon him and with his stripes we are healed. All we like sheep have gone astray; we have turned every one to his own way, then the Lord has laid on him the iniquity of us all" (Isa. 53:5-6).

In simplest terms, this then is the doctrine of the Atonement: God's Son died for the sins of His people.

I want to lift up two aspects of this doctrine about which there is disagreement among Christians—two facets of the Presbyterian and Reformed position that are disputed: It was specific and it was effective.

Specific Atonement

First, it was and is *specific* atonement. Some call it *definite atonement*. It was designed specifically for the benefit of Christ's people, i.e., for those whom the Father had given to the Son.

On the night before His crucifixion, Jesus instituted the Lord's Supper as a memorial to His death. In giving it He said, "This is my body which is broken for you," and "This is my blood shed for many for the remission of sins." He was speaking, of course, of His dying on the cross. And then He offered what we call His great high-priestly prayer recorded in John 17, in which He tells us clearly *for whom* His sacrificial intercession was intended. "Father," he said, "I have finished the work You gave me to do"—anticipating that on the following day just before He died He would say, "It is finished." So now He prays, "Father, I have finished the work You gave me to do; I have made known Your words to *those whom You gave me out of the world*. They were Yours, and You gave them to me. Keep by Your power *those whom You have given me*. Neither do I pray for these alone but for all those who shall believe on me through their words . . . Father, I pray that *those whom You have given me* shall be with me where I am that they may behold my glory."

Six times in His prayer Jesus speaks of "those whom the Father has given me." This passage and others in the New Testament make it clear that there is a company of people—unknown to us and unknowable by us, but known to the Father and the Son. They constitute His people, His elect. And the atonement wrought by Christ on Calvary was specifically for them.

Theologians used to call it *limited* atonement—a misleading term. It is not limited in its ability to accomplish what God intended. It is not limited in its power to save to the uttermost all who come to God by faith. But, its benefits are limited to those who believe—to those who are called by God to faith in His Son. Your faith in Jesus Christ marks you as a member of that company whom the Father has given to the Son and for whom Christ died.

It was and is specific or limited atonement.

Effective Atonement

The second facet that I would highlight is that it was and is *effective* atonement It effectually accomplished what the Father and the Son intended, namely: full atonement for the sins of God's people.

Some Christians hold that on the cross the penalty for sins was potentially but not effectively paid. They hold that Christ's death provided a kind of blanket amnesty for everybody, a general but conditioned pardon which makes forgiveness possible but not actual. Christ's atoning work, they hold, is not complete without our faith.

Those who hold this position believe that salvation is in part our own doing; they do not believe that we are fully and effectively delivered from sin by the grace of God alone. So, they offer a redemption that does not fully redeem and a Savior who does something less than save.

Over against that position, we affirm the finished nature of Christ's sacrificial work. As the writer of the Book of Hebrews says, "Christ obtained eternal redemption for us" (9: 12)—obtained it, not merely made it possible. Paul uses several phrases in Romans 5 which show the finished nature of Christ's work on the cross for us. He says that we are "justified *by his blood*" (v. 9); we have been "reconciled to God *by the death of His Son*" (v. 10);

and "through the Lord Jesus Christ we have *now* received the atonement" (v. 11). Jesus Himself said, "It is finished."

My faith in Christ does not complete His work of atonement. That is finished. My faith merely appropriates for me the benefits of His completed work. Saving faith is faith in a finished atonement. One cannot be saved by believing what is not a fact. If Christ's atonement did not fully pay the penalty for all my sins, my meager faith certainly cannot do it.

So, Christ's sacrificial death on the cross—His atonement—was and is *specific, limited,* and *effective.* It was specifically designed for and limited to those whom the Father had given to the Son; and it effectively accomplished their salvation.

Now, if one does not believe this doctrine, he must be ready to bear the weight of his own guilt, ready to atone for his sins the best way he can.

But the joy of this doctrine—and here I come to its personal application—the joy of this doctrine is that I now know, and so can you, that Christ on the cross paid in full the penalty for all my sins. The check that Jesus wrote in His blood on Calvary had my name written on it—and yours too if you believe His word. On the Day of Judgment (and there will surely be such a day), there will be a Bill of Indictment against me. All my sins will be listed there; and it will be a long list! But since Calvary there has been written across the face of my bill: PAID IN FULL.

> Jesus paid it all. All to Him I owe.
> Sin had left a crimson stain;
> He washed it white as snow.

Because of the atonement wrought by Christ on Calvary, my salvation is forever settled and sure; and so is yours, if you believe God's Word.

So, we do not wonder what will happen to us at the Judgment. We can say with Paul, "There is therefore no condemnation to them which are in Christ Jesus" (Rom. 8:1). That is good news! That is the heart of the Gospel! With that confidence we can go on our way rejoicing!

Chapter Five

The Grace of God

The most popular hymn in this country today is "Amazing Grace." In a recent poll of over ten thousand persons representing thirty-two different denominations, "Amazing Grace" was far ahead of all other hymns.

The surprising thing is how popular this hymn is among non-religious groups. We often hear it sung by rock groups and civic choruses. I believe one reason it is so popular among non-religious groups is that it does not mention the name of Jesus Christ. It can be seen as broadly religious without being confined to the Christian faith. It appeals to a kind of vague religiosity that is popular in this country today. But I have the uncomfortable feeling that many who sing this hymn never listen to the words beyond the first line: "Amazing grace, how sweet the sound." The next three lines declare that I am a "wretch" who was lost and blind until I was found. Many persons who sing this great hymn would never admit that they were lost souls that needed to be found. Nor do they have any idea what the second verse means when it says, "'Twas grace that taught my heart to fear / And grace my fears relieved."

The German pastor Dietrick Bonhoeffer, who, because of his resistance to Hitler, was put to death by the Nazis during World War II, spoke of the prevalence of "cheap grace": grace without responsibility, grace

41

without any cost to man or God. Cheap grace. Many persons with whom this hymn is popular are acquainted only with cheap grace.

So, I want us to examine the grace of God from a biblical perspective.

And to guide our thinking, I have chosen the text from Ephesians 2:8. *"By grace are you saved through faith, and that not of yourselves; it is the gift of God."*

There are four key words in this text and we shall examine them in succession.

The first word is *saved.*

Saved

"By grace you are saved." This is the most important word in the text because all the others point to it. But what does it mean to be *saved?* Many people are turned off by the word; when the preacher mentions it, they tune him out. Some Christians are prejudiced against it because they connect it with a style of evangelism that rubs them the wrong way.

But it is a good biblical word for which there is no substitute.

And whether we realize it or not, each one of us wants to be saved. There is a longing in the soul of each person—a wistful yearning after something—and he is not sure what it is that he wants.

There is a story in my wife's family about a small cousin called "Baby Jo." One day she was especially unhappy and restless; no activity or toy satisfied her. Finally Baby Jo asked her grandmother, who spoiled her, "Ganny, what Baby Jo want?" Poor child, she didn't know what she wanted; she was just unhappy and "wanted."

But ask rebellious teenagers, "What do you want?" and they don't know. Ask business executives who, after being given a coveted promotion, are still restless, "What do you want?" and they don't know. Poor Pete Rose (and I can't claim any kin with him) had fame and a winning record, a good job and plenty of money, but still was not satisfied. "Pete, what do you want?" "I don't know."

We are all striving for something. All religions are efforts to satisfy the longing; politics and culture are fueled by the yearning. What is it? The Christian faith calls it *salvation*. What do they want—the rebellious teenager, the disillusioned executive, the unhappy ball player? They want a salvation that satisfies their souls. They want fulfillment, wholeness. They want what the Bible calls "Shalom"—peace. They want to be *right* with themselves and with their fellows and with God. They want salvation!

It will help to understand the biblical concept of salvation if we remember that, theologically, *saved* is a categorical term. It allows no modifiers. It is either fact or it is not. One is either saved or not. There is no half-way ground, no such thing as being a little bit saved.

It is like being pregnant (if you will excuse my use of the illustration). A woman is either pregnant or not. There is no such thing as being a little bit pregnant. But, salvation, like pregnancy, does have a past tense, a present tense, and a future tense. A woman might say, "I became pregnant during the third week in January." Past tense. She might say, "I am pregnant." Present tense. She may even say to another woman, "My pregnancy is not so advanced as yours," but both are now pregnant. Still present tense. And a woman might say, "My pregnancy will come to fullness in October when I am delivered." Future tense.

In the same way, we can speak of biblical salvation. We can say, "I have been saved ever since Christ died for my sins and I came to believe." Past tense. We can say, "I am being saved as the Holy Spirit brings me along the road to sanctification." Present tense. And we can say, "I will be saved when I see my Lord face to face." Future tense. Most of us here have been saved, for we believe in Christ as Savior and Lord. Past tense. Most of us are being saved, for we are striving to grow in the Christian life. Present tense. And most of us will be saved when we are delivered from the body of this death and given a new body. Future tense.

Salvation is what we all long for!

But, how is one saved? The text says, "By grace."

Grace

"By grace are you saved." Grace is the second key word in the text. And remember: it is *God's* grace, not ours. There are three facets to God's grace: His favor, His mercy, His power.

Grace is *favor*. Unmerited affection. An illustration is the love of a mother for her baby. The baby has not earned the mother's favor; indeed, the baby has caused the mother only pain and sleepless nights. Yet the mother showers unmerited affection on the child. That is grace as unearned favor.

In like manner, God's grace is His unmerited love for sinners. This grace is for *all* persons. It is sometimes called *common* grace, or general grace, meaning that it is poured out upon everyone. This grace sends the rain and the sunshine on the just and the unjust. This grace provides numerous blessings for those who do not love God as well as for those who do. Grace as unmerited favor.

Then, there is grace as mercy or *forgiveness*. This is *special* grace which God shows to His own, to those who believe in Jesus Christ. He forgives their sins, treats them with special favor and provides them with particular blessings. Grace as forgiveness.

Then, there is grace as *power*. Power to believe. Power to resist temptation. Power to live a Christian life. Says the hymn, "'Twas grace that taught my heart to fear / And grace my fears relieved." That is grace as power.

So it is by grace that we are saved. It is by God's mercy and power that we come to salvation—to wholeness, to the satisfaction and joy and peace for which we long. It is God Who *has* and *is* and *will* save us by His grace.

Now, the text says that we are saved "through faith."

Faith

"By grace are you saved through faith." Faith is the third key word.

What is faith? Faith is confident trust in a person that leads to action. It is believing that what a person has said, he will do; that what he has promised, he will fulfill, and acting on that person's word. A father tells his young son, "I'll take you to the beach Saturday." Believing him, the son begins to collect the things he wants to take to the beach and lives all week in joyous anticipation. A mother says to her daughter, "This morning I deposited $200 in your bank account. You may write checks on it for clothes for going away." If the daughter has faith in her mother, she will write checks up to $200 with confidence. In each case, faith in the parents' word brings blessings to the son and the daughter. The children, by believing, appropriate the benefits promised because they have acted on their faith.

The Bible tells us that God called Abraham in the land of Ur and said to him, "I am going to bless you and be a God unto you and to your seed after you. I'm going to make your name great and give you the land of Canaan for an inheritance." Now, it was not for anything that Abraham had done that God gave him this promise.

The promise came from the unmerited grace of God. And the record says, "And Abraham believed God," so he gathered his family and his flocks together and set out for the land of Canaan. Abraham was confident that the One who had promised was trustworthy, so he acted on that faith. Thus Abraham became an example of faith and the father of the faithful.

The promise of God to Abraham is renewed again and again in the Old and New Testament. On the Day of Pentecost, Peter said to the people, "The promise (What promise? The promise to Abraham!) is unto you and unto your children."

So, God says to you and me today, just as he said to Abraham: "I am going to bless you and save you; I'm going to be a God unto you and to your children after you; I'm going to keep you in all your pilgrim way and bring you at last to myself--to the Promised Land." And those who believe God's Word, count Him trustworthy who promised, and act as if His Word is true, they begin immediately to receive the blessings of God's salvation: the forgiveness of their sins, the joys and satisfactions of knowing God as their Father. He becomes their God; He keeps them and gives them all things needful, and He brings them at last to Heaven when their work on earth is done.

Christian faith is reliance on God for salvation through Jesus Christ. "By grace are you saved through faith," that is, through trusting His promise and then acting on that promise.

There is one more word in the text: "By grace are you saved through faith, and that not of yourselves, it is the gift of God." The fourth word is *gift*.

Gift

Here is a biblical truth which some Christians have

not grasped. Here is a disputed element of Calvinism. Calvinists hold that saving faith is a *gift* of God; that God gives us the power to believe. Some Christians hold that faith is something that they conjure up in their own hearts. They hold that "believing" is something that *they* do—a work. But Presbyterians hold that faith is a gift of God, that God gave us the power to believe. As the hymn says, "'Twas grace that *taught* my heart to fear." God's grace worked faith in my heart.

When Paul preached in Philippi, a woman named Lydia heard him and the record says, "whose heart the Lord opened" so that she believed (Acts 16:14). After Peter had confessed Jesus, saying, "Thou are the Christ, the Son of the Living God," Jesus said to him, "Flesh and blood did not reveal this to you, but my Father which is in heaven." God gave Peter the power to believe. Faith is a gift.

Faith is like sleep; it cannot be willed. You cannot fall asleep by an act of your will. Indeed it seems sometimes that the harder you try to sleep, the more sleep flees from you. Sleep is accomplished by surrounding yourself with those things that are conducive to sleep: quietness, a comfortable position, eyes closed, mind centered on happy things. You *can* control your surroundings, but sleep is a gift. Faith is like that. You cannot believe by an act of your will. You cannot simply say, "I'm going to believe that the moon is made of green cheese" and start believing it. And one cannot believe that the Bible is the Word of God or that Jesus is God's Son by simply saying, "I'm going to believe that." But one can choose the company of those who believe these things; one can read in the Scriptures and elsewhere of men and women who had faith; one can ask God to give him or her faith—and He will. But, in the final analysis, faith is a gift from God.

So, if you believe in Jesus Christ; if you are trusting

Him for salvation, then, thank God for that faith for it was His gift to you. Then pray that "He, which hath begun a good work in you will perform it until the day of your salvation." Thank God that you *have been, are now,* and *will be* saved through faith which was His gift, and then set yourself with determination to confirm that faith by a life of purity and of service to others. Let your prayer be the words of the hymn:

> Come, Thou Fount of every blessing,
>   Tune my heart to sing Thy grace;
> Streams of mercy, never ceasing,
>   Call for songs of loudest praise.
> Teach me some melodious sonnet,
>   Sung by flaming tongues above;
> Praise the mount! I'm fixed upon it,
>   Mount of God's unchanging love.
>
> Here I raise my Ebenezer,
>   Hither by Thy help I'm come;
> And I hope, by Thy good pleasure:
>   Safely to arrive at home,
> Jesus sought me when a stranger
>   Wandering from the fold of God;
> He, to rescue me from danger,
>   Interposed His precious blood.
>
> Oh to grace how great a debtor
>   Daily I'm constrained to be!
> Let that grace now, like a fetter,
>   Bind my wandering heart to Thee.
> Prone to wander, Lord, I feel it,
>   Prone to leave the God I love;
> Here's my heart, oh take and seal it,
>   Seal it for Thy courts above.

What a great text! "By grace you are saved through faith, and that not of yourselves, it is the gift of God."

Saved by grace through faith which is a gift from God—that is the heart of the Christian faith.

Chapter Six

Irresistible Grace

For what are you *most* grateful? Of all the blessings which you have, for what are you the most thankful?

I am grateful for my wife, for my parents, for my children, for the privilege of ministering in this fine congregation. I am thankful for a degree of health and for educational opportunities. I am grateful that I am an American, a Southerner, a North Carolinian. I have so many things to be thankful for!

But I am *most* grateful *that I am a Christian*—that I know myself to be, through Jesus Christ, a child of God.

For this blessing to whom should I be grateful? Who is responsible for my being a Christian? My mother, my father, a teacher, a friend? Perhaps. They were instruments. But who moved them to do what they did? God! It was my heavenly Father who initiated the process, and He has continued it until this moment. And by whose power can any of us hope to complete the journey and come at last to heaven? Speaking for myself, I know that I will never make it without God's unfaltering help.

The main point of this sermon is that you and I are Christians, that we are in the Kingdom of God, by the grace of God alone, and when we join that happy throng before the throne of God in heaven, our song will be, "Only a sinner, saved by grace."

So, our topic is: the doctrine of irresistible grace.

This doctrine declares that our salvation from beginning to end is the work of God alone. My hope in this sermon is to enable us all to grasp with our hearts as well as with our minds the full import of what this doctrine teaches, so that gratitude will prompt us to a fresh resolve to live a life that is pleasing to God and that confirms our salvation.

There are three adjectives which theologians have used to define God's grace. They are: *prevenient, irresistible,* and *invincible.* Each adjective identifies a slightly different facet of God's saving activity.

Prevenient

It is called prevenient grace—*grace that comes before.* The English word *prevenient* comes from two Latin words: *pre* meaning "before," and *veni* meaning "to come." Prevenient grace is grace which comes before or precedes. In the saving activity of God it precedes faith. Your faith in Christ was not something which you aroused in your own heart. As we said previously: faith is a gift.

Some Christians think that they just decided to believe in Christ and so started doing so. The truth is that to believe is never an act of one's will. You cannot one morning just resolve that you are going to believe something and then do so. Unlike the White Queen in *Alice in Wonderland,* we cannot draw a long breath, shut our eyes, and believe six impossible things before breakfast.

Suppose a neighbor should say to you, "Ten elephants slept last night in my kitchen." Seeing your skeptical look, she would add, "Please believe me.'" But you cannot believe her by an act of your will. You can be convinced (note the passive voice: be convinced) by evidence or by the testimony of trustworthy witnesses, but you cannot just say, "I'm going to believe" and then start

51

believing. Believing is not a matter of your will.

George is a high school senior. On several occasion he has given his parents accounts of events which they learned later from other parents were not entirely correct. Now George wants permission and money for another excursion. His account of what is planned does not ring true: his parents are skeptical and they hesitate. George says, "I wish you would believe me!" They love him and would really like to believe him, but they can't do it by just deciding to. They *can* decide to give him the money in spite of their doubts, but they cannot just decide to believe.

Faith comes from outside ourselves. We can put ourselves in a position to be convinced. We can listen to the testimony of trustworthy witnesses. But faith is a gift. New Christians sometimes say, "I gave my heart to Christ." We rejoice in what has happened to them but their description is not quite accurate because it suggests that "I" did it all by myself. It would be more correct for one to say, "The Holy Spirit convicted me of my need of a Savior and led me to accept Christ."

Jesus said, "No man can come to me, except the Father which hath sent me draw him" (John 6:44). To the Corinthians the apostle Paul wrote, "No one can say that Jesus is Lord but by the Holy Spirit" (I Cor. 12:3). And John in his first epistle wrote, "We know that the Son of God . . . has given us an understanding that we may know him" (1 John 5:10).

Saving grace is prevenient grace. It comes to us first and initiates faith in our hearts.

Irresistible

Another adjective used to describe God's grace is irresistible. One of the five disputed points of Calvinism is the doctrine of irresistible grace.

Let no one cling to an erroneous impression of *irresistible* as applied to God's saving activity. God does not bring anyone into the Kingdom against his or her will. God is not a bulldozer that runs roughshod over anyone regarding salvation. God's grace is not irresistible in the way an avalanche of snow is irresistible to a mountain climber. These are not the ways in which God's grace is irresistible.

But, Peter likens becoming a believer to a birth. To believers the apostle wrote, "You have been born anew . . . by the Word of God" (1 Peter 1:23). A fetus in a womb does not resist the grace that would give it birth. Paul wrote to the Christians in Ephesus, "We are His workmanship, created in Christ Jesus" (Eph. 2:10). The clay with which the potter is working does not resist the grace that would make it a vase. Again to the Ephesians the apostle wrote, "You hath He quickened who were dead in trespasses and sins" (Eph. 2:1). A man who is dead, whose heart has stopped beating, does not resist the grace of the physician or the man from the Rescue Squad who, either by massage or shock, would start his heart pumping again. The corpse, the vase, and the baby have neither the desire nor the power to resist. *That* is the way God's grace is irresistible.

As birth to a fetus, as formation to a vase, as quickening to a dead man—so God's grace was irresistible to us.

Here we must make a distinction between *common* grace and *saving* grace. Common grace is *not* irresistible. This is the general favor which God shows to all persons. This grace causes the rain to fall and the sun to shine on unbelievers as well as believers. God offers numerous blessings through nature, through society, through culture, and these blessings are available to all; and anyone can accept or reject them. Common grace can be, and often is, resisted.

But, when saving grace worked faith in our hearts and brought us to salvation, we had neither the will nor the power nor the wish to resist.

This saving, irresistible grace may come in countless ways. It may come subtly, quietly, as it did to Timothy from his mother and his grandmother. This is the way it came to most of us here. But it may come in some dramatic experience, as it did to the apostle Paul and to Martin Luther—both were knocked down on the road by a terrifying encounter. God's saving grace may come through people. It may come through words spoken or written. It may come through events like a sickness or an accident or the birth of a child. God's saving grace comes in countless ways, and in none of them do we have the wish to resist.

So, the grace of God is prevenient and it is irresistible.

Invincible

Finally, God's grace is termed as invincible. It always accomplishes what God intends.

Our forefathers in the Reformed faith called it *effectual calling*. The *Westminster Confession of Faith* describes it thus:

> All those whom God had predestined unto life . . . He is pleased, in His appointed time, to call by His Word and Spirit . . . out of that state of sin and death into salvation . . . enlightening their minds to understand . . . things of God . . . renewing their wills, and by His almighty power determining them to that which is good, and effectually drawing them to Jesus Christ; yet so as they

come freely, being made willing by His grace (chap. 12).

Here again we must make a distinction; between the external call, on the one hand, and the internal call, on the other. The external call is not invincible. Jesus cried, "Come unto me all ye that labor and are heavy laden, and I will give you rest" (Matt. 11:28). Many who heard that call did not come. They ignored the invitation. In the parable of the great feast, Jesus told of a man who provided a feast and sent his servants to call his friends to the banquet, but his friends did not come. The external call to the gospel is not invincible. To sound this external invitation is one of the main tasks of the church. Jesus said, "Go ye into all the world and preach the gospel to every creature" (Mark 16:15). As Christians we are to broadcast the invitation to all persons everywhere for we do not know in whom the Lord by His Spirit will work faith. So, the external call is our responsibility.

But the internal call is God's work. And the Bible says clearly that "Many are called, but few are chosen" (Matt. 22:14). The internal call in the human heart is the work of the Holy Spirit. This inner call is effectual; it always accomplishes what God intends. Jesus said, "All that the Father gives me shall come to me" (John 6:37).

So, the grace of God is prevenient, effectual, invincible.

We conclude, therefore, that our salvation, our being and continuing in the Kingdom of God, was and is the work of God from beginning to end. Our proper response is gratitude, and a diligent effort to live a Christian life.

Let this, then, be our prayer. "Thank You, Father, for making me Your child. Thank You for working faith in my heart. And thank You for bringing me 'through many dangers, toils and snares.' Although I have slipped and fallen repeatedly; although I am often tempted to leave You, continue, I pray, to sustain me in the faith until the end, and enable me more and more to live a life that is pleasing to You—a life that shows my gratitude and confirms my salvation." God grant that that shall be our constant prayer.

For the aim of God's prevenient, irresistible, invincible grace is life in Christ for you and me.

Chapter Seven

Perseverance of the Saints

No doctrine is able to bring more joy to the heart of a believer than this one—sometimes called the *doctrine of eternal security* or popularly described as *blessed assurance*. Few blessings are greater than the assurance that your life, your soul, is safe with God; that your "name from the palm of His hand / Eternity cannot erase; / Impressed on His heart it remains / In marks of indelible grace." No person is more joyous than the one who knows that he or she is being "kept by the power of God . . . unto salvation ready to be revealed in the last time" (1 Peter 1:5).

As we look at this doctrine, it is my hope that this joy will come to you.

A Definition of the Doctrine

The doctrine declares that once God has begun the work of salvation in any person, He will persevere therein to the end and will never let any of His own be lost. Since the Bible teaches that faith is a *gift* of God, this doctrine simply declares that God never takes back what He gives. Once He gives faith, He never takes it back but continues to nourish and sustain it. As the apostle Paul says, "The gifts and call of God are irrevocable." (Rom. 11:29)

This doctrine is sometimes defined as "Once saved,

always saved," but I have never liked that definition because it leaves God out of the process, and makes the security of the believer automatic. And there is nothing automatic about it; we are "kept by the power of God." Even the term "perseverance of the saints" is misleading. Saints do not do the persevering, but God does. It should be called "The Preservation of the Saints," for it is God who preserves us to the end.

An illustration of contrast may help. One can hold either to the cat or the monkey doctrine of how salvation is accomplished for or by believers. A mother cat, wishing to move her kittens, grasps the kitten firmly by the nape of the neck in her mouth and carries the little one where she will. In stark contrast, the poor baby monkey must grab hold of the mother's fur and hold on for dear life. As the mother monkey swings through the trees, the little monkey must hold on tightly or fall. Those persons who hold the monkey doctrine believe that they have hold of God and it's all up to them to hold on. Those who hold the cat doctrine believe, as the doctrine of the perseverance of the saints teaches, that God has hold of them and He will never let go.

Those who hold the cat doctrine can sing with meaning the lines from "Amazing Grace" which declare: "Through many dangers, toils and snares / I have already come 'Tis grace has brought me safe thus far, / And grace will lead me home." They hear God saying to them as another hymn affirms:

> The soul that on Jesus hath leaned for repose,
> I will not, I will not desert to his foes;
> That soul though all hell should endeavor to shake
> I'll never, no never, no never forsake.

This doctrine is firmly rooted in the Scriptures.

Firmly Rooted in the Scriptures

Jesus said, "My sheep hear my voice, and I know them and they follow me, and I give them eternal life, and they shall never perish, neither shall anyone snatch them out of my hand. My Father which gave them to me is greater than all and no one is able to snatch them out of my Father's hand" (John 10:29). And again He said, "This is the will of my Father who hath sent me, that of all whom He hath given me I should lose none, but should raise them up at the last day" (John 6:39).

The apostle Paul wrote to the Philippians, "I am sure that He who began a good work in you will bring it to completion at the day of Jesus Christ" (1:6). And to the Corinthians he wrote, "Our Lord Jesus Christ . . . will sustain you to the end . . . for God is faithful, by whom you were called into the fellowship of His Son" (I Cor. 1:8-9). To the Ephesians the apostle wrote, "You are sealed unto the day of redemption" (4:30), "sealed by the Holy Spirit of promise" (1:13). If you want to make something secure, you seal it. So Paul says believers have been sealed by the Holy Spirit until the day of their final redemption.

To quote again from 1 Peter:

> Elect according to the foreknowledge of God . . . Who . . . hath begotten us unto a lively hope by the resurrection of Jesus Christ from the dead, to an inheritance incorruptible and undefiled and that fadeth not away, reserved in heaven for you who are kept by the power of God through faith unto salvation to be revealed at the last time. (1:2-5).

Believers are safe in the hands of God unto the end.

Some Problems and Questions

One problem is posed by church members who fall away—persons who, at one time, expressed faith in Christ and joined the church and worked in it, but then lost interest and fell away. Do these persons give the lie to this doctrine? No, they do not. Such persons can be divided into two groups. On the one hand are back-sliding Christians who fall away temporarily but eventually return to the faith. Like the Prodigal Son in the parable who went away from the father but in the end returned, so these believers lose heart for a time but return. On the other hand are persons who never really believed, and so were never in the faith. Like Judas whose heart was never really with the Lord, their real interests were in the world, and back to the world they went.

We know a great deal about back-sliding Christians for most of us have experienced, in some degree, doubts and loss of zeal. Most of us, like David and Peter, have sinned and denied our Lord at some time or another. But God draws us back, forgives us, and restores us to place in His family. One great preacher has likened these persons to a sailor on a ship in a storm. The sailor may be knocked down on the deck by the waves and the rolling of the ship, but he is never washed overboard. He always rises and continues to work. Believers may have doubts and fall into sin, but God never deserts His own, and by His grace they persevere to the end.

On the other hand there are those persons who never really believed. Like Judas their heart was never in it. For a time they went through the motions and said all the right words, but they never really came to believe or to surrender to the Lord. Jesus said, "Not every one that saith unto me, Lord, Lord, shall enter the kingdom of heaven" (Matt. 7:21). And John in his first epistle speaks of certain persons who "went out from us, but they were not of us for if they had been of us they would have continued with us" (1 2:19). These persons serve as a warning that we must "Be diligent that we may be found in Him" (2 Peter 3:14).

Another question posed by this doctrine is: Will the acceptance of this doctrine cause a person to be less cautious about how he or she lives? Will it lead some to say, "Hey, man, I've got it made! I can do as I please!" The obvious answer is that anyone who speaks or acts in that way demonstrates, beyond the shadow of all doubt, that he does not have a true faith, but has a spurious counterfeit. Anyone who says, "I can do as I please" does not possess a saving faith that will bring him to heaven but possesses a false faith that can secure a spot in hell.

By our deeds we confirm our faith. By our efforts to live a Christian life, we show that our faith is genuine. Says John, "Everyone that hath this hope in him purifieth himself, even as He is pure" (1 John 3:3).

Which leads us to ask:

How this Doctrine Works

Just how does it affect the one who believes it? I said that no doctrine is able to bring more joy to the believing heart; I said that there are few blessings greater than the blessed assurance that your life, your soul, is safe in God's hands. How so? Why does this bring joy? Let me answer with a story.

Marsha was a quiet, lovable little girl of seven years when both her parents died. She was sent to live with her only living relative, her Aunt Jane. But, after less than a year, Aunt Jane had a stroke and had to be put in a nursing facility, and Marsha became a ward of the state. She was placed in a foster home where both the parents drank heavily and an older boy bullied her. She was given little love. She tried hard to do what her foster parents wanted, but she could never please them. What they seemed to want most was the money that they received for her support.

The social worker assigned to Marsha's case realized that the child was not developing but was withdrawing into herself, so she found what appeared to be a more responsive pair of foster parents. But that hope proved futile too. Again Marsha tried to please them but they expected more than the child was able to do. She was so unhappy. At school she heard the other girls talking about their homes and their parents, and she longed for a home of her own where she would *belong* and feel secure and loved. But she knew her real parents were dead, and so she felt that such could never happen. Many nights she cried herself to sleep.

Bob and Nan Conner had lost a little girl to leukemia and came to the agency seeking a child to adopt. When Marsha and the Conners saw each other, it was love at first sight. In their home were all that Marsha had longed for: two caring parents, a room with a bed of her own, and enough things to keep her busy. When the adoption papers were completed, Bob and Nan had sense enough to show the documents to Marsha and to explain to her the meaning of the pages with all the signatures on them. They explained that these documents meant that she was now *their* little girl, that they were truly her parents—her very own—and that she was no longer in a foster home, temporarily—this was her home *for keeps*.

From that day, Marsha blossomed. She smiled, she sang, she began to do well in school, she was a different child. What had happened? She had been given a sense of security. She belonged for keeps. She was no longer on probation. She could now get on with the business of growing up—of being loved and loving. Being good was now a joy and not a burden—not something she *had* to do but something she *wanted* to do.

So it is with us. The Bible speaks of our *adoption* as children of God. And once God has adopted us, He will never *unadopt* us. So we can have a sense of security. We belong to God for keeps—forever and forever. Now we can get on with the business of growing in the Christian life. Now living a Christian life is something we want to do, not something we must do to win God's favor.

As the old hymn says: "When I can read my title clear / To mansions in the skies, / I'll bid farewell to every fear / And wipe my weeping eyes."

This then is the doctrine of the perseverance of the saints, the doctrine of eternal security: Once God has begun the work of salvation in any child of His, He will persevere therein to the end and will never let any of His own be lost. Henceforth they are "kept by the power of God unto salvation, ready to be revealed at the last time," because "He that hath begun a good work in you will perform it until the day of Jesus Christ."

A Warning

But always with this doctrine the Scriptures sound a strong word of warning: "Let him that thinketh that he standeth, take heed lest he fall" (1 Cor. 10:12). Again, "Work out your own salvation with fear and trembling, for it is God which worketh in you both to will and to do His good pleasure" (Phil. 2:12-13). And again, "Be diligent to make your calling and election sure" (1 Peter 1:10). Make your calling and election sure! Not that you need to convince God that you are His child—He knows *that* since He chose you; but you need to convince yourself that you are His child, to confirm the fact in your own heart, and to demonstrate it to the world.

When we confirm our salvation by a life that glorifies God and serves other people, we can have that "blessed assurance" that our names are written indelibly in the Lamb's Book of Life. Then we can go on our way rejoicing.